Teddy's Socks

February 27, 1919

It was a cold Thursday in February, and today a baby boy with a fiery spirit was born.

His parents put on Teddy's little socks to keep his fire inside.

November 1, 1929

Teddy is 10 years old and is working to bring money home. It was the start of the Great Depression, and money was hard to come by.

Every day, Teddy puts on his holey socks and worn-out shoes to go collect aluminum cans and glass bottles. He walks across town to bring them to Tick's Recycling, a new business that pays for old metal and glass. Teddy can get a few cents for each bottle he brings in.

When Teddy gets home, he pulls himself up to the countertop and reaches behind his mother's large bowl of spoons. His hand finds the top of the glass Ball jar that was hiding from sight. He pulls it toward him and brings all the change he got from recycling that day to the top of the jar.

It wasn't a whole lot of money, but it would help get him, Gladys, Evie, and Everett some new socks for the winter ahead.

September 15, 1940

Teddy is now 21, and he has become a hardworking young man. It is his wedding day, so he puts on his nice socks and shoes and drives over to his love's house. They take a drive to Missouri and get married there. They work hard to buy an itty-bitty green home with lots of land around it, making sure to hide a small glass jar on the counter, behind the large jar of spoons.

JUST
Married

Marriage License
STATE OF MISSOURI
SEAL OF THE SECRETARY OF STATE
MISSOURI
That Theodore C. Streenz of Normal
and Ruth M. Ethington of Bloomington
were by me joined together in holy matrimony.
September 15, 1940

Certificate of Completion
awarded to
Theodore C Streenz

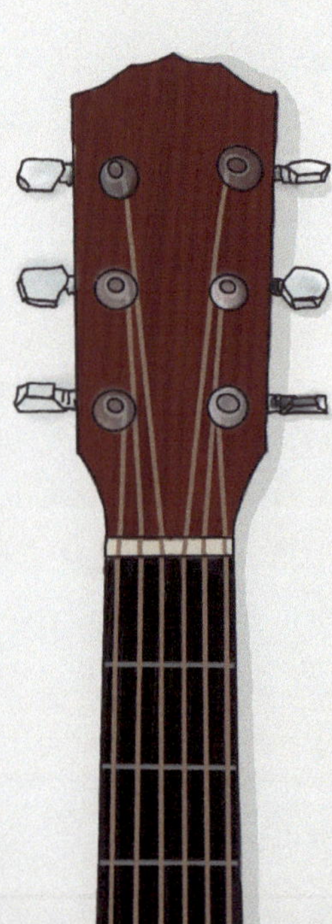

Over the following years, Teddy has had many jobs. He knows how to do just about everything under the sun. He is a guitar player, a carpenter, a mechanic, and even a bus driver. Anything he sets his mind to, he can do.

Dec 24, 1955

Teddy and Ruth are up wrapping gifts for four little pairs of feet (two more little feet to come). They have worked hard all year to make sure their kids get something they need for Christmas. So, it is time for them to pull out the daily newspaper and wrap the socks, sweaters, and hats that the kids will get in the morning.

news today
THE BLOOMINGTON RECORD

Dec 24, 2008

Many years and many more little feet later...

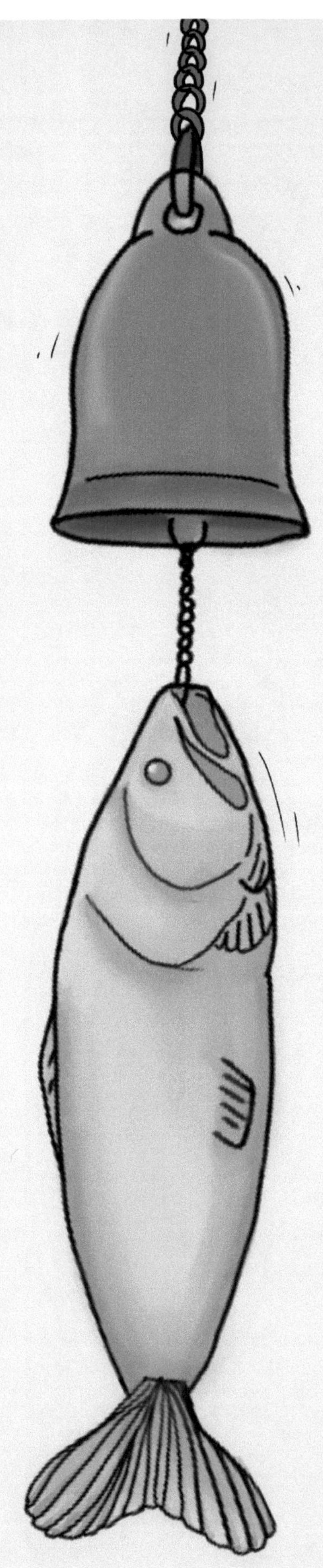

'Grandpa, it's me, Tim!' yelled Teddy's grandson, banging his head on the fish chime above the door of the itty-bitty green house. The chime was always ready to warn Teddy of someone arriving.

'Timmy! It's good to see you!' smiled Teddy.

'Oh, there's my honey!' he chuckled when he saw the small brown-haired girl hiding behind her father. She smiles and ducks her head back behind her father's leg.

Teddy holds out his arms, and the little girl runs in for a hug, giving her great-grandfather a kiss on the cheek.

It was Christmas Eve, and Teddy had wrapped all the presents by himself, thinking of Ruth the whole time. He had a lot more socks to gift than when they first started out. Now, there were five kids, twelve grandkids, and many, many great-grandchildren that Teddy got to give to.

Oh, and that old glass jar still sat behind the spoons on the counter, still saving for the ones he loved.

'This one's for you,' smiled Teddy brightly, handing a medium-sized package wrapped in the daily newspaper to the timid little girl.
Although she already knows what it will be, because he gets everyone he loves the same thing, she is excited to receive a gift from her great-grandpa Teddy.

Author's Note

That little girl always wondered why her great-grandpa only gave out socks, and even more, why they were wrapped in newspaper. But after many years of sitting and listening to her great-grandfather's stories, she finally understood. The season of giving is much more about the love and care someone has to give than the physical gift. Even better, the gift you give can be meaningful and useful, not just about having the newest things. Teddy always gave his loved ones what they needed; from a word to a hand, he was always there to model what hard work and perseverance looked like. Theodore Carl Streenz Sr. was the inspiration for this book. He was my great-grandfather, who grew up as a small boy during the Great Depression. He lived to be 95 and was the best storyteller and gift-giver of all time.